family ci

*Classic
Essential*

∾ ✿ ∾

Puddings

The Family Circle® Promise of Success

Welcome to the world of Confident Cooking, created for you in the
Family Circle® Test Kitchen, where recipes are double-tested by our team
of home economists to achieve a high standard of success.

MURDOCH BOOKS®

Sydney • London • Vancouver • New York

~ Pudding Power ~

After making your first pudding, you'll wonder why you hadn't made one before. A few simple techniques are all you need to master these delicious puddings. No longer confined to the steamed variety, they can range from simple fruit crumbles to a rich fruit-filled Christmas pud—whatever the choice, there will always be a pudding to satisfy everyone.

Bowls and Basins

We have used a variety of different shapes and sizes of bowls and basins throughout this book, to show the versatility of the pudding.

Measure the capacity of your basin or dish with water, by filling it as close to the top as possible. If a basin is too small you might find your pudding will burst at its seams!

The depth of a dish is usually determined by the type of pudding. For instance, if we used a deep soufflé dish for a bread and butter pudding, there would only be a small layer of bread covering the top—how would you stop the family fighting over the delicious crusty topping?

Steaming

Many of the most traditional puddings are the steamed variety.

The two most popular pudding steamers available are either metal or ceramic. The metal steamer is generally made from aluminium and comes with a lid which is secured to the base with small clips. This is attached after the paper and foil have been secured around the rim. The ceramic basins do not have lids, so must be covered equally tightly with paper and foil and tied with string to ensure they won't let in any water.

Due to the thickness of the ceramic, cooking times are slightly longer in ceramic basins than metal. We have used ceramic throughout this book, so if you are using metal you will need to reduce the time slightly.

Preparing the basin

Some puddings may stick to the bottom of the basin. In addition to greasing well, it is a good idea to place a round of baking paper onto the base. After spooning in the mixture, level the top to ensure an even surface.

Preparing the saucepan

Place a trivet or a small old saucer in the base of a saucepan large enough to hold the pudding basin

Place the trivet in the base of a large saucepan.

comfortably. Sit the basin on the trivet and add enough water to come halfway up the side of the basin. Remove the basin and place the water on to boil.

Preparing the paper

Place a sheet of foil on the work surface and top with a sheet of baking paper. Make a wide pleat through the centre, ensuring both the paper and foil are in the pleat. This fold gives room for the pudding to rise, while still keeping it airtight.

Fold a pleat in the centre of the foil and paper.

Brush the paper with melted butter.

Place the paper and foil, buttered-side-down, over the pudding in the basin and tie round the rim with string. Tie an extra couple of lengths of string to either side of the basin and use these as a handle to lower the pudding into the boiling water. You will need to

Lower the prepared basin, using the string handles.

reduce the heat now so the water is simmering when you put the lid on. Ensure the water is only halfway up the side of the basin—if it is too high, water may work its way in and spoil the pudding.

Steaming the pudding
Once the pudding is in the pan, cover with a tight-fitting lid and

simmer according to the recipe. Keep an eye on the water level—it may be necessary to top up the water every hour. Always use boiling water and pour down the outside of the basin. This is so the pudding doesn't lose temperature while cooking. Adding cold water would be like opening the oven halfway during baking a cake. When the recommended time is up, pierce through the layers of paper and foil with a skewer to check if it is cooked. If the skewer comes out sticky, cook a little longer and test again. Leave for 5 minutes, or more if specified, before turning out. This allows the pudding to firm slightly.

Some of the large puddings can be made into individual servings. Cook these in smaller metal or ceramic moulds in the oven and don't forget to reduce the cooking time. Small puddings are best cooked in a water bath. This method steams the puddings rather than baking them, giving a more moist result.

A Substitution Racket

Substituting fruits like stewed peaches or quinces for other fruits,

such as the apples in the crumble or Eve's Pudding, is totally acceptable throughout this book—providing the fruits are of a similar consistency—so use whatever's in season. Similarly, various types of bread such as panettone, raisin bread or brioche may be used instead of plain bread in dishes like Bread and Butter Pudding. And if you love the strong flavour of citrus, you can increase the amount of rind without affecting the outcome of the pudding.

Tricks of the Trade

~For best results, always have your ingredients at room temperature—especially the butter and eggs. If you do add cold eggs to a creamed butter and sugar mixture, it will look like the mixture has curdled. But don't panic—the batter will blend together once the flour has been added.

~When pouring liquid over the top of uncooked batter (for instance when making a self-saucing pudding) it is a good idea to pour the liquid over the back of a spoon. This ensures the liquid is evenly spread out, without leaving a hole in the mixture.

~ Chocolate ~
Self-saucing Pudding

Preparation time:
10 minutes
Total cooking time:
40 minutes
Serves 6

1 cup (125 g)
self-raising flour
1 tablespoon cocoa
powder
1/2 cup (125 g) caster
sugar
1 egg
1/2 cup (125 ml) milk

60 g butter, melted
1 teaspoon vanilla
essence
1 cup (250 g) caster
sugar, extra
2 tablespoons sifted
cocoa powder, extra

1 ~ Preheat the oven to moderate 180°C (350°F/Gas 4). Brush a deep 2 litre ovenproof dish with melted butter.

2 ~ Sift the flour and cocoa into a large bowl, add the sugar and stir until combined. Make a well in the centre.

3 ~ In a jug, whisk the egg and add the milk, melted butter and vanilla essence. Pour the liquid into the well in the dry ingredients and, using a wooden spoon, stir the mixture until well combined. Pour into the ovenproof dish.

4 ~ Combine the extra sugar and the extra cocoa in a small bowl and sprinkle evenly over the pudding mixture. Gently pour 1 1/2 cups (375 ml) boiling water over the back of a spoon onto the pudding mixture. Bake for 30–40 minutes, or until a skewer comes out clean when inserted into the centre of the cake only—a sauce will have formed underneath. Serve immediately with cream or ice cream.

NUTRITION PER SERVE
Protein 6 g; Fat 10 g;
Carbohydrate 80 g; Dietary
Fibre 1 g; Cholesterol 58 mg;
1830 kJ (437 cal)

Variation ~ Self-saucing puddings can be made using a variety of flavourings for added interest. For a jaffa flavour, add a couple of teaspoons of finely grated orange rind to the egg and milk mixture. Or for a mocha flavour, add 1–2 teaspoons of instant coffee to the dry ingredients.

Combine the sifted flour and cocoa powder in a large mixing bowl and add the sugar.

Pour the liquid ingredients into the well in the centre of the dry ingredients.

Slowly pour boiling water over the back of a spoon onto the pudding mixture.

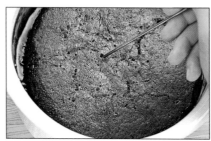

The pudding is cooked when a skewer inserted into the cake comes out clean.

~ Lemon Delicious ~

Preparation time:
20 minutes
Total cooking time:
35 minutes
Serves 4

60 g unsalted butter	¹/₃ cup (40 g)
³/₄ cup (185 g) caster	self-raising flour
sugar	¹/₄ cup (60 ml) lemon
3 eggs, separated	juice
1 teaspoon finely grated	³/₄ cup (185 ml) milk
lemon rind	icing sugar, to dust

1⁓Preheat the oven to moderate 180°C (350°F/Gas 4). Grease a deep 1 litre ovenproof dish with melted butter.
2⁓Beat the butter, sugar, egg yolks and rind until light and creamy. Add the sifted flour and stir until just combined. Stir in the juice and milk.
3⁓Beat the egg whites in a small, dry bowl until stiff peaks form. Fold into the flour mixture with a metal spoon until just combined.
4⁓Spoon into the ovenproof dish and place in a deep baking dish. Pour in enough boiling water to come halfway up the side. Bake for 35 minutes, or until golden brown. Dust with icing sugar to serve.

NUTRITION PER SERVE
Protein 7.5 g; Fat 20 g; Carbohydrate 55 g; Dietary Fibre 0.5 g; Cholesterol 180 mg; 1710 kJ (410 cal)

Add the flour to the egg and butter mixture and stir until just combined.

Beat the egg whites in a small bowl until stiff peaks form.

Fold the egg whites into the flour mixture with a metal spoon until just combined.

Pour boiling water into the baking dish to come halfway up the side.of the dish.

~ Queen of Puddings ~

Preparation time:
25 minutes +
10 minutes standing
Total cooking time:
55 minutes
Serves 6

2 cups (500 ml) milk 1 cup (80 g) fresh white breadcrumbs 2 eggs, separated 1/3 cup (90 g) sugar	2 tablespoons strawberry jam 100 g strawberries, sliced

1. ~Preheat the oven to moderate 180°C (350°F/Gas 4). Brush a shallow 1 litre ovenproof dish with melted butter.

2. ~Heat the milk in a medium pan until it almost boils and the surface has a wrinkled appearance. Remove the pan from the heat. Place the breadcrumbs in a large bowl, pour on the hot milk and leave for 10 minutes. Beat the egg yolks with half the sugar and stir into the breadcrumb mixture.

3. ~Spoon the custard into the ovenproof dish and bake for 45 minutes, or until firm.

4. ~Combine the jam and sliced strawberries and spread evenly over the cooked custard. Beat the egg whites in a clean dry bowl until stiff peaks form, then beat in the remaining sugar to make a meringue. Swirl the meringue over the top of the strawberries with a palette knife. Increase the oven temperature to hot 220°C (425°F/Gas 7) and bake for 3–4 minutes, or until the meringue is set and lightly browned. Serve the Queen of Puddings hot or warm.

NUTRITION PER SERVE
Protein 7 g; Fat 5.5 g;
Carbohydrate 33 g; Dietary
Fibre 1 g; Cholesterol 70 mg;
850 kJ (205 cal)

Notes. ~Always beat egg whites in a clean dry bowl. Any hint of grease in the bowl or yolk in the egg whites will prevent the egg whites foaming. To beat to 'stiff peaks' means that when the beaters are removed from the egg whites the peaks will stand up straight without folding over. For more volume when making meringue, use eggs that are a couple of days old. Bring them to room temperature before beating.

Heat the milk until it is almost boiling and the surface has wrinkled.

Swirl the meringue over the strawberry and jam mixture.

~ Jam Puddings ~

Preparation time:
30 minutes
Total cooking time:
50 minutes
Serves 6

---

185 g unsalted butter,
  softened
3/4 cup (185 g) caster
  sugar
1 teaspoon vanilla
  essence

3 eggs, lightly beaten
1/2 cup (60 g) plain flour
1 cup (125 g)
  self-raising flour
1/2 cup (160 g) berry
  jam

---

1 ~ Preheat the oven to moderate 180°C (350°F/ Gas 4). Lightly grease six 1 cup (250 ml) heatproof moulds with melted butter. Cover the bases with small rounds of baking paper.

2 ~ In a large bowl, beat the butter, sugar and vanilla essence until light and creamy. Add the beaten eggs gradually, beating well after each addition. Using a metal spoon, fold in the combined sifted flours, a quarter at a time.

3 ~ Spoon the mixture evenly into the moulds and smooth the surface. Cover each mould with a piece of greased foil, pleated in the middle. (The pleat allows the pudding to expand during cooking.) Secure with string. Place the moulds in a large deep baking dish. Pour in enough boiling water to come halfway up the sides of the moulds. Bake for 45 minutes, or until a skewer inserted into the centre of each pudding comes out clean.

4 ~ Put the jam in a small pan and stir over low heat for 3–4 minutes, or until it forms a warm liquid.

5 ~ Leave the puddings for 5 minutes before loosening the sides with a knife and turning out onto serving plates, then remove the paper. Serve the puddings topped with a spoonful of the jam and with custard, cream or ice cream.

NUTRITION PER SERVE
Protein 6.5 g; Fat 30 g; Carbohydrate 70 g; Dietary Fibre 1.5 g; Cholesterol 170 mg; 2325 kJ (555 cal)

Variation ~ Any flavoured berry jam can be used—try strawberry, blackberry or raspberry.
Note ~ Cooking in a water bath steams the puddings rather than baking them, giving a more moist result.

Lightly grease individual moulds and cover each base with baking paper.

Fold in the combined flours with a metal spoon, a quarter at a time.

Cover the moulds with greased foil, pleated down the centre, and secure with string.

Pour boiling water into a baking dish to come halfway up the sides of the moulds.

~ Apple Charlotte ~

Preparation time:
40 minutes
Total cooking time:
55 minutes
Serves 8

1.6 kg cooking apples, peeled, cored and sliced	3 strips of lemon rind
	1 cinnamon stick
	80 g unsalted butter
1/2 cup (125 g) caster sugar	1 loaf sliced white bread, crusts removed

1 Cook the apple, sugar, rind, cinnamon stick and 30 g butter over low heat, stirring occasionally, until tender but not mushy. Remove the rind and cinnamon.
2 Preheat the oven to moderately hot 200°C (400°F/Gas 6). Grease a 1.25 litre charlotte tin or pudding basin.
3 To line the tin, cut 4 slices of bread in half diagonally, then cut one edge off each triangle with a round cutter to fit the base. Cut wide strips of bread to line the side. Leave enough bread to cover the top. Spread the bread with the remaining butter and line the tin, butter-side-down.
4 Spoon the apple into the tin. Cover with the remaining bread and bake for 30–40 minutes, or until golden.

NUTRITION PER SERVE
Protein 1 g; Fat 8.5 g; Carbohydrate 40 g; Dietary Fibre 4 g; Cholesterol 25 mg; 1015 kJ (240 cal)

Cook the apple mixture over low heat until the apples are tender.

Cut one edge off each bread triangle with a round cutter to make them fit the base.

Butter each slice of bread, then line the mould butter-side-out.

Fill with apple mixture and cover with the remaining bread slices.

～ Sussex Pond Pudding ～

Preparation time:
20 minutes
Total cooking time:
4 hours
Serves 4–6

2³/4 cups (340 g)
  self-raising flour
170 g suet or butter,
  frozen
1/3 cup (80 ml) milk

250 g unsalted butter,
  cut into cubes
1 cup (220 g) demerara
  sugar
1 thin-skinned lemon

1.～Grease a 1.5 litre pudding basin with melted butter. Place a round of baking paper in the base.

2.～Place the empty basin in a large pan on a trivet or upturned saucer and pour in enough cold water to come halfway up the side of the basin. Remove the basin and put the water on to boil.

3.～Sift the flour into a large bowl and grate the frozen suet into the flour. Mix into the flour, then mix in the milk and 160 ml water, using a flat-bladed knife until just combined. Bring together with your hands.

4.～Reserve one-quarter of the pastry for the lid. Roll out the rest on a lightly floured surface into a 25 cm circle, leaving the middle thicker than the edge. Press into the basin leaving a little bit above the rim.

5.～Put half the butter and half the sugar in the basin. Prick the lemon all over with a skewer and place in the middle of the basin, then top with the rest of the butter and sugar. Fold the edge of the pastry into the bowl and brush with water. Roll the reserved pastry out to cover the basin and press firmly onto the rim of the pastry to seal.

6.～Lay a sheet of foil on the work surface and cover with a sheet of baking paper. Make a large pleat in the middle. Grease the paper with melted butter. Place, paper-side-down, across the top of the basin and tie string securely around the rim of the basin and over the top of the basin to make a handle. The string handle is used to lift the pudding in and out of the pan.

7.～Gently lower the basin into the simmering water and cover with a tight-fitting lid. Cook for 4 hours. Check the level of water every hour and top up to the original water level with boiling water as needed.

8.～To serve, leave the pudding to stand for 5 minutes before turning out onto a plate with a rim. When the pudding is cut, the combination of sugar, butter and lemon juice will flow out to form the 'pond'. Serve with slices of the lemon and cream.

NUTRITION PER SERVE (6)
Protein 6.5 g; Fat 60 g; Carbohydrate 80 g; Dietary Fibre 2.5 g; Cholesterol 130 mg; 3685 kJ (880 cal)

Notes～ A traditional English pudding and a speciality of Sussex, this can also be known as 'well' pudding. Suet is traditional in this recipe, although butter can be substituted, if preferred. On standing, this pudding will continue to absorb the 'pond' and the base and side will thicken.

Press the pastry into the basin, leaving a little extra over the rim.

Put half the butter and sugar in the basin and add the pierced lemon.

～ Cherry Clafoutis ～

Preparation time:
15 minutes
Total cooking time:
35 minutes
Serves 6–8

500 g fresh cherries, or 800 g can pitted cherries	25 g unsalted butter, melted
2 eggs, lightly beaten	$1/2$ cup (60 g) plain flour
1 cup (250 ml) milk	$1/3$ cup (90 g) sugar
	icing sugar, to dust

1～Preheat the oven to moderate 180°C (350°F/Gas 4). Brush a shallow 1 litre ovenproof dish with melted butter.
2～Remove the pits from the cherries and spread in the dish in a single layer. If using canned cherries, drain thoroughly and spread out on paper towels to absorb any excess juices before spreading in the dish. If they are still wet, they will leak into the batter.
3～ Combine the beaten eggs, milk and the melted butter in a large jug. Sift the flour into a large bowl, add the sugar and make a well in the centre. Gradually add the egg mixture to the dry ingredients, whisking until smooth and free of lumps. Transfer to a large jug.
4～ Pour the batter gently over the cherries and bake for 30–35 minutes. The batter should be risen and golden around the cherries. Remove from the oven and dust generously with icing sugar. Serve immediately.

NUTRITION PER SERVE (8)
Protein 5 g; Fat 5.35 g; Carbohydrate 35 g; Dietary Fibre 2.65 g; Cholesterol 57 mg; 852 kJ (204 cal)

Notes～ A clafoutis (pronounced 'clafootee') is a classic French batter pudding, and is a speciality of the Limousin region. Clafoutis comes from 'clafir', a dialect verb meaning 'to fill'. It is traditionally made with cherries, although blueberries, raspberries, blackberries or small, well-flavoured strawberries, can be used as an alternative. Use a shallow pie dish to ensure the top cooks to a delicious golden brown. If canned cherries are difficult to obtain, halved pitted canned plums make a good substitute.

Make a well in the centre of the dry ingredients in the bowl.

Gently pour the batter over the cherries in the ovenproof dish.

~ Pineapple ~ Upside-down Cake

Preparation time:
30 minutes
Total cooking time:
1 hour
Serves 6–8

90 g butter, melted
1/2 cup (95 g) soft brown sugar
440 g can pineapple rings in natural juice
6 red glacé cherries
125 g butter, chopped
3/4 cup (185 g) caster sugar
1 teaspoon vanilla essence
2 eggs
1 1/2 cups (185 g) self-raising flour
1/2 cup (60 g) plain flour
1/3 cup (30 g) desiccated coconut

1 ~ Preheat the oven to moderate 180°C (350°F/ Gas 4). Pour the melted butter into a 20 cm round tin, and brush some of it over the base and side of the tin, leaving most on the base. Sprinkle the brown sugar over the base. Drain the pineapple, reserving 1/2 cup (125 ml) of the juice. Arrange the pineapple rings over the base of the tin—five around the outside and one in the centre. Place a cherry in the centre of each pineapple ring.
2 ~ Using electric beaters, beat the butter, caster sugar and vanilla essence together until light and creamy. Add the eggs one at a time, beating well after each addition.
3 ~ Sift the flours onto the creamed mixture, and add the coconut and reserved juice. Fold in with a metal spoon or rubber spatula until just combined. Spoon the mixture evenly over the pineapple and smooth the surface. Indent the centre of the mixture with the back of a spoon to ensure the cake has a flat surface when it has been cooked.
4 ~ Bake the cake for 50–60 minutes, or until a skewer comes out clean when inserted into the centre of the cake. Leave the cake in the tin for 10 minutes, before turning out to serve.

NUTRITION PER SERVE (8)
Protein 5.32 g; Fat 25 g; Carbohydrate 67 g; Dietary Fibre 2.5 g; Cholesterol 115 mg; 2150 kJ (515 cal)

Arrange five pineapple rings around the base of the tin and one in the middle.

Indent the centre of the mixture to ensure the cake has a flat surface when cooked.

~ Ginger Pudding ~

Preparation time:
30 minutes
Total cooking time:
1³/4–2 hours
Serves 6–8

2 tablespoons finely
  chopped glacé ginger
185 g butter
³/4 cup (140 g) lightly
  packed soft brown
  sugar
3 eggs

2 tablespoons golden
  syrup
¹/2 cup (60 g) plain flour
1 cup (125 g)
  self-raising flour
1 tablespoon ground
  ginger
¹/4 teaspoon mixed spice

1.~Grease the base and side of a 1.5 litre pudding basin with melted butter. Place a round of baking paper in the base.

2.~Place the empty basin in a large pan on a trivet or upturned saucer and pour in enough cold water to come halfway up the side of the basin. Remove the basin and put the water on to boil.

3.~Sprinkle the chopped ginger in the bottom of the basin.

4.~Beat the butter and sugar together until light and creamy. Add the eggs one at a time, beating well after each addition, then beat in the golden syrup—the mixture may look curdled at this stage.

5.~Fold the sifted flours and spices into the butter mixture with a large metal spoon. Spoon the mixture into the basin over the ginger.

6.~Lay a sheet of foil on the work surface and cover with a sheet of baking paper. Make a large pleat in the middle. Grease the paper with melted butter. Place, paper-side-down, across the top of the basin and tie string securely around the rim of the basin and over the top of the basin to make a handle. The string is used to lift the pudding basin in and out of the pan.

7.~Gently lower the basin into the simmering water and cover with a tight-fitting lid. Cook for 1³/4–2 hours, topping up the water as necessary.

8.~Remove the basin from the water. Leave for 5 minutes. Turn out onto a serving plate and serve with whipped cream or warm custard.

NUTRITION PER SERVE (8)
Protein 5 g; Fat 20 g;
Carbohydrate 42 g; Dietary
Fibre 1 g; Cholesterol 125 mg;
1545 kJ (370 cal)

Line the base of a greased pudding basin with a round of baking paper.

Sprinkle the chopped ginger evenly in the bottom of the basin.

Using a metal spoon, fold the sifted flours and spices into the butter mixture.

Use the string handle to lower the pudding basin into the pan of water.

～ Treacle Pudding ～

Preparation time:
30 minutes
Total cooking time:
2 hours
Serves 4–6

5 tablespoons golden
   syrup
4 tablespoons treacle
185 g butter, softened
3/4 cup (185 g) caster
   sugar

1 teaspoon vanilla
   essence
3 eggs
1/2 cup (60 g) plain flour
1 cup (125 g)
   self-raising flour

1.～Grease the base and side of a 1.5 litre pudding basin with melted butter. Place a round of baking paper in the bottom of the basin.
2.～Place the empty basin in a large pan on a trivet or upturned saucer and pour in enough cold water to come halfway up the side of the basin. Remove the basin and put the water on to boil.
3.～Pour 2 tablespoons golden syrup and 1 tablespoon treacle into the basin. Beat the butter, sugar and vanilla essence with electric beaters until light and creamy. Add the eggs, the sifted flours and

another tablespoon of treacle and beat on low speed until combined. Spoon into the basin, levelling the top.
4.～Lay a sheet of foil on the work surface and cover with a sheet of baking paper. Make a large pleat in the middle. Grease the paper with melted butter. Place, paper-side-down, across the top of the basin and tie string securely around the rim of the basin and over the top of the basin to make a handle. This is used to lift the basin in and out of the pan.
5.～Gently lower the basin into the simmering water and cover with a

tight-fitting lid. Cook for 2 hours, topping up with boiling water when necessary.
6.～Remove from the pan and test with a skewer or by pressing the top gently—the pudding should be firm in the centre and well risen. If not cooked, simply re-cover and cook until done. Leave for 5 minutes before turning out. Warm the remaining golden syrup and treacle and pour over the pudding to serve.

NUTRITION PER SERVE (6)
Protein 5.5 g; Fat 27 g; Carbohydrate 70 g; Dietary Fibre 1 g; Cholesterol 140 mg; 2260 kJ (540 cal)

Using electric beaters, beat the butter and sugar until light and creamy.

Spoon the pudding mixture into the basin and level the top.

Make a large pleat across the centre of the baking paper and foil.

The pudding is cooked when the centre is firm to the touch and well risen.

～ Sweet Potato Pudding ～

Preparation time:
25 minutes
Total cooking time:
1 hour 5 minutes
Serves 4–6

2 large orange sweet
  potatoes (about 1 kg)
4 eggs
³/₄ cup (140 g) lightly
  packed soft brown
  sugar
¹/₂ teaspoon ground
  cinnamon

¹/₄ teaspoon ground
  nutmeg
large pinch ground
  cloves
¹/₄ teaspoon ground
  allspice
1 cup (250 ml) milk
icing sugar, to dust

1.～Peel and chop the orange sweet potatoes into even-sized pieces. Steam or microwave for 10–15 minutes, or until tender (don't boil in lots of water or your mash will be too wet). Mash well until smooth, then leave to cool.
2.～Preheat the oven to moderate 180°C (350°F/Gas 4). Lightly grease a

1.5 litre ovenproof dish with melted butter.
3.～Whisk the eggs and sugar in a large bowl until thick and pale. Stir in the cinnamon, nutmeg, cloves, allspice, milk and sweet potato until well combined. Pour into the dish.

4.～Bake the pudding for 45–50 minutes, or until a skewer inserted into the centre comes out clean. Serve hot, dusted with icing sugar.

NUTRITION PER SERVE (6)
Protein 8.7 g; Fat 5 g; Carbohydrate 50 g; Dietary Fibre 3 g; Cholesterol 126 mg; 1150 kJ (275 cal)

～ Traditional Rice Pudding ～

Preparation time:
10 minutes
Total cooking time:
2 hours
Serves 4

¹/₄ cup (55 g) short-
  grain rice
1²/₃ cups (410 ml) milk
1¹/₂ tablespoons caster
  sugar
³/₄ cup (185 ml) cream

¹/₄ teaspoon vanilla
  essence
¹/₄ teaspoon freshly
  grated nutmeg
1 bay leaf

1.～Preheat the oven to slow 150°C (300°F/Gas 2). Grease a 1 litre shallow ovenproof dish with melted butter.
2.～Mix together the rice, milk, caster sugar, cream and vanilla essence and pour into

the dish. Dust with the freshly grated nutmeg and float the bay leaf on top.
3.～Bake the rice pudding for 2 hours, by which time the rice should have absorbed most of the milk and be

creamy in texture with a brown skin on top. Remove the bay leaf before serving.

NUTRITION PER SERVE
Protein 5.3 g; Fat 25 g; Carbohydrate 25 g; Dietary Fibre 0.30 g; Cholesterol 75 mg; 1358 kJ (325 cal)

Sweet Potato Pudding (top), Traditional Rice Pudding.

~ Summer Pudding ~

Preparation time:
30 minutes
+ overnight refrigeration
Total cooking time:
5 minutes
Serves 6

150 g blackcurrants
150 g redcurrants
150 g raspberries
150 g blackberries
200 g strawberries,
hulled and quartered
or halved

1/2 cup (125 g) caster
sugar, or to taste
6–8 slices good-quality
sliced white bread,
crusts removed

1.~Put all the berries except the strawberries in a large pan with $1/2$ cup (125 ml) water and heat gently for 5 minutes, or until the berries begin to collapse. Add the strawberries and remove from the heat. Add sugar, to taste (how much you need will depend on how ripe the fruit is). Cool.

2.~Line a 1 litre pudding basin or six $2/3$ cup (170 ml) moulds with the bread. For the large mould, cut a large circle out of one slice for the bottom and cut the rest of the bread into wide fingers. For the small moulds, use one slice of bread for each, cutting a circle to fit the bottom and strips to fit snuggly around the sides. Drain a little of the juice off the fruit mixture. Dip one side of each piece of bread in the juice before fitting it, juice-side-down, into the basin, leaving no gaps. Do not squeeze or flatten the bread or it will not absorb the juices.

3.~Fill the centre of the basin with the fruit and add a little juice. Cover the top with the remaining dipped bread, juice-side-down, trimmed to fit. Cover with plastic wrap. Place a small plate which fits inside the dish onto the plastic wrap, then weigh it down with heavy cans or a glass bowl. Place on an oven tray to catch any juices which may overflow the basin. For the small moulds, cover with plastic and sit a small can, or a similar weight, on top of each. Refrigerate overnight. Carefully turn out the pudding and serve with any leftover fruit mixture and cream.

NUTRITION PER SERVE
Protein 5 g; Fat 1.5 g; Carbohydrate 45 g; Dietary Fibre 7.5 g; Cholesterol 0 mg; 910 kJ (215 cal)

Heat the berries, except the strawberries, until they begin to collapse.

Place slices of bread, juice-side-down, into the basin.

Cover the berry-filled basin with juice-dipped bread and cover with plastic wrap.

Place a small plate over the basin, on top of the plastic wrap.

~ Steamed Christmas Pudding ~

Preparation time:
20 minutes
Total cooking time:
7 hours
Serves 12–16

375 g fresh suet	1¹/2 cups (280 g)
6 cups (480 g) fine fresh	chopped mixed peel
breadcrumbs	8 eggs, lightly beaten
4¹/2 cups (560 g) raisins	²/3 cup (170 ml) brandy
1²/3 cups (250 g)	extra brandy, for
currants	lighting

1 ~ Grease a 2 litre pudding basin with melted butter. Place a round of baking paper in the base. Place the empty basin in a large pan on a trivet or upturned saucer and pour in enough cold water to come halfway up the side of the basin. Remove the basin and put the water on to boil.

2 ~ Remove the membrane from the suet and discard. Grate the suet finely either by hand or in a food processor. Transfer to a very large mixing bowl. Add the breadcrumbs, raisins, currants and mixed peel and mix until they are thoroughly combined.

3 ~ Add the eggs to the fruit mixture and mix well. Gradually add the brandy and combine thoroughly. Spoon the mixture into the basin.

4 ~ Lay a sheet of foil on the work surface and cover with a sheet of baking paper. Make a large pleat in the middle. Grease the paper with melted butter. Place, paper-side-down, across the top of the basin and tie string securely around the rim of the basin and over the top of the basin to make a handle. Gently lower the basin into the boiling water using the handle and cover with a tight-fitting lid. Cook for 7 hours. Check the level of water and top up with boiling water as needed. Leave for 10 minutes before turning out onto a shallow flameproof serving dish.

5 ~ If you want to prepare beforehand and reheat, leave in the basin and steam, as above, for 2 hours. Heat a little extra brandy, pour over the pudding and ignite. Serve with brandy butter, cream, or custard.

NUTRITION PER SERVE (16)
Protein 7.5 g; Fat 25 g; Carbohydrate 60 g; Dietary Fibre 4.5 g; Cholesterol 105 mg; 2108 kJ (505 cal)

Remove the membrane surrounding the suet and discard.

Add the eggs to the fruit mixture and mix until well combined.

Make a large pleat across the centre of the baking paper and foil.

Tie string securely around the rim of the basin and over the top to make a handle.

~ Bread and Butter Pudding ~

Preparation time:
20 minutes
+ 30 minutes soaking
+ 1 hour refrigeration
Total cooking time:
40 minutes
Serves 4

1/2 cup (60 g) mixed
  raisins and sultanas
2 tablespoons brandy or
  rum
30 g butter, softened
4 slices good-quality
  white bread or
  brioche loaf
3 eggs

1/4 cup (60 g) caster
  sugar
3 cups (750 ml) milk
1/4 cup (60 ml) cream
1/4 teaspoon vanilla
  essence
1/4 teaspoon ground
  cinnamon
1 tablespoon demerara
  sugar

1.~Soak the raisins and sultanas in the brandy or rum for 30 minutes. Butter the slices of bread or brioche and cut each piece into 8 triangles. Arrange the bread in a 1 litre shallow ovenproof dish.

2.~Beat the eggs, sugar, milk, cream, vanilla and cinnamon in a large jug. Add the raisins, sultanas and any liquid and mix well.

3.~Pour the custard over the bread. Make sure the fruit is spread out evenly. Cover and refrigerate for 1 hour.

4.~Preheat the oven to moderate 180°C (350°F/Gas 4). Sprinkle the pudding with the demerara sugar. Bake for 35–40 minutes, or until the custard is set and the top is crunchy and golden.

NUTRITION PER SERVE
Protein 14 g; Fat 24 g; Carbohydrate 54 g; Dietary Fibre 1.5 g; Cholesterol 200 mg; 2106 kJ (503 cal)

Notes~It is very important that you use good-quality bread in a bread and butter pudding. Ordinary sliced white bread will tend to go a bit claggy when it soaks up the milk. Bread and butter pudding can be made with all sorts of bread or cake leftovers. Croissants, Danish pastries, panettone and fruit loaf make luscious bread and butter puddings. A sprinkling of demerara sugar or crushed sugar cubes will give a lovely crunchy topping. For a shiny top, glaze the hot pudding with warmed apricot jam.

Soak the raisins and sultanas in the brandy for 30 minutes.

Arrange the triangles of bread in the ovenproof dish.

Pour the custard mixture evenly over the top of the bread.

Sprinkle the top of the pudding with demerara sugar.

～ Sticky Date Pudding ～

Preparation time:
15 minutes
+ 15 minutes soaking
Total cooking time:
45 minutes
Serves 8

1 cup (185 g) chopped,
  pitted dates
1 teaspoon bicarbonate
  of soda
90 g butter, softened
1/2 cup (115 g) firmly
  packed soft brown
  sugar
1 teaspoon vanilla
  essence
2 eggs, lightly beaten

1 1/2 cups (185 g)
  self-raising flour

Sauce
1 cup (230 g) firmly
  packed soft brown
  sugar
1 cup (250 ml) cream
90 g butter
1/2 teaspoon vanilla
  essence

1. ～Preheat the oven to moderate 180°C (350°F/Gas 4). Brush a deep 18 cm square cake tin with melted butter and line the base with baking paper.
2. ～Put the dates and bicarbonate of soda in a medium heatproof bowl and add 1 cup (250 ml) boiling water. Stir and leave for 15 minutes.
3. ～Using electric beaters, beat the butter, sugar and vanilla until light and creamy. Gradually add the eggs, beating well after each addition. Fold in half of the sifted flour, then half of the date mixture. Stir in the remaining flour and the remaining dates, mixing until well combined.
4. ～Pour the mixture into the cake tin and bake for 40 minutes, or until a skewer comes out clean when inserted into the centre of the pudding. Leave the pudding in the tin to cool for 10 minutes before turning out.
5. ～To make the sauce, put the sugar, cream, butter and vanilla essence in a small pan and bring to the boil, stirring. Simmer the sauce over low heat for 5 minutes. Pour over the pudding and serve with whipped cream.

NUTRITION PER SERVE
Protein 5 g; Fat 33 g; Carbohydrate 75 g; Dietary Fibre 3 g; Cholesterol 145 mg; 2532 kJ (605 cal)

Notes ～The cake can be frozen for up to three months. This is equally delicious using apricots in place of the dates.

Pour boiling water onto the dates and bicarbonate of soda.

Stir in the remaining flour and the dates until well combined.

～ Orange Marmalade Pudding ～

Preparation time:
20 minutes
Total cooking time:
1 1/2 hours
Serves 4

1 thin-skinned navel
  orange
90 g butter, softened
1/2 cup (125 g) caster
  sugar
2 eggs

1/3 cup (105 g) chunky
  orange marmalade
2 teaspoons finely
  grated orange rind
2 cups (250 g)
  self-raising flour
1/3 cup (80 ml) milk

1. ～ Grease the base and side of a 1.25 litre pudding basin with melted butter. Place a round of baking paper in the bottom of the basin.

2. ～ Place the empty basin in a large pan on a trivet or upturned saucer and pour enough cold water to come halfway up the side of the basin. Remove the basin and put the water on to boil.

3. ～ Remove the skin and pith from the orange by cutting off the top and bottom and cutting downwards all the way round. Slice the orange thinly, place one slice in the bottom of the basin and arrange the others around the side.

4. ～ Beat the butter and sugar until light and creamy. Add the eggs, one at a time, and beat well. Stir in the marmalade and rind, then add the sifted flour and mix thoroughly. Stir in the milk and spoon the mixture into the prepared basin without disturbing the orange slices.

5. ～ Lay a sheet of foil on the work surface and cover with a sheet of baking paper. Make a large pleat in the middle. Grease the paper with melted butter. Place, paper-side-down, across the top of the basin and tie string securely around the rim of the basin and over the top of the basin to make a handle. The string handle is used to lift the pudding in and out of the pan.

6. ～ Gently lower the basin into the simmering water and cover with a tight-fitting lid. Cook for 1 1/2 hours. Check the level of water and top up with boiling water as needed. Turn out onto a plate to serve.

NUTRITION PER SERVE
Protein 10 g; Fat 20 g;
Carbohydrate 65 g; Dietary
Fibre 3 g; Cholesterol 150 mg;
2095 kJ (500 cal)

Remove the skin and pith of the orange by cutting downwards.

Slice the orange thinly and arrange slices around the side of the pudding basin.

Spoon the mixture carefully on top of the orange slices in the basin.

Using the string handle, lower the pudding basin into the water.

∼ Golden Syrup Dumplings ∼

Preparation time:
15 minutes
Total cooking time:
30 minutes
Serves 4

1 cup (125 g)
  self-raising flour
40 g butter, chopped
1 egg, lightly beaten
1 tablespoon milk

Syrup
1 cup (250 g) sugar
40 g butter, chopped
2 tablespoons golden
  syrup
¼ cup (60 ml) lemon
  juice

1∼Sift the flour into a bowl, add the butter and rub in until the mixture resembles breadcrumbs. Mix in the combined egg and milk with a flat-bladed knife to form a soft dough.
2∼To make the syrup, put 2 cups (500 ml) water in a pan with the sugar, butter, syrup and lemon juice. Stir over medium heat until dissolved.
3∼Bring to the boil and gently drop in dessertspoons of the dough. Cover and reduce the heat to a simmer. Cook for 20 minutes, or until a knife inserted into a dumpling comes out clean. Serve immediately, drizzled with syrup.

NUTRITION PER SERVE
Protein 5 g; Fat 18 g; Carbohydrate 96 g; Dietary Fibre 1.2 g; Cholesterol 97 mg; 2327 kJ (556 cal)

Rub the butter into the flour, using just your fingertips.

Stir in the egg and milk mixture with a flat-bladed knife to form a soft dough.

Gently drop dessertspoons of the dough into the golden syrup mixture.

The dumplings are cooked when a knife inserted into the centre comes out clean.

～ Plum Cobbler ～

Preparation time:
25 minutes
Total cooking time:
35 minutes
Serves 4

750 g plums, halved
  and stones removed
  (or use canned plums,
  drained, syrup
  reserved)
1/3 cup (90 g) caster
  sugar
1 teaspoon vanilla
  essence

Topping
1 cup (125 g)
  self-raising flour
60 g butter, chopped
1/4 cup (55 g) firmly
  packed soft brown
  sugar
1/4 cup (60 ml) milk
1 tablespoon caster
  sugar

1 ～ Preheat the oven to moderately hot 200°C (400°F/Gas 6). Grease a shallow 1.5 litre ovenproof dish.
2 ～ Put the plum halves, sugar and 2 tablespoons water into a pan and bring to the boil, stirring until the sugar dissolves. (If using canned plums add 1/3 cup (80 ml) of the syrup at this stage instead of using the sugar and the water.)
3 ～ Simmer the plums, covered, for 5 minutes, or until they are tender, then slip the skins off if you like. Add the vanilla essence and spoon the mixture into the dish.
4 ～ To make the topping, sift the flour into a large bowl and add the butter. Using your fingertips, rub the butter into the flour until it resembles fine breadcrumbs. Stir in the brown sugar and 2 tablespoons of milk. Using a flat-bladed knife, mix to form a soft dough, adding a little more milk if necessary. Turn onto a lightly floured surface and gather together to form a smooth dough. Roll out until the dough is 1 cm thick and cut into rounds with a 4 cm cutter.

5 ～ Arrange the rounds over the plum filling, overlapping around the side. (The plums in the middle of the dish will not be covered.) Lightly brush the rounds with the remaining milk and sprinkle with the caster sugar. Place the dish on a baking tray and bake for 30 minutes, or until the topping is golden brown and cooked through.

NUTRITION PER SERVE
Protein 5 g; Fat 13 g; Carbohydrate 78 g; Dietary Fibre 5.5 g; Cholesterol 40 mg; 1884 kJ (450 cal)

Roll out the dough to a 1 cm thickness and cut into rounds with a 4 cm cutter.

Overlap the rounds of dough, over the plum filling, around the side of the dish.

~ Spotted Dick ~

Preparation time:
15 minutes
Total cooking time:
1 1/2 hours
Serves 4

125 g fresh suet
1 1/3 cups (165 g)
  plain flour
1 1/2 teaspoons
  baking powder
1/2 cup (125 g)
  caster sugar
1 1/2 teaspoons
  ground ginger
2 cups (160 g) fresh
  white breadcrumbs
1/2 cup (60 g) sultanas
3/4 cup (110 g) currants
2 teaspoons finely
  grated lemon rind
2 eggs, lightly beaten
2/3 cup (170 ml) milk

1 ~ Remove the membrane from the suet and discard. Grate the suet by hand or use a food processor. Sift the flour, baking powder, sugar and ginger into a large bowl. Add the breadcrumbs, sultanas, currants, suet and rind and mix well.

2 ~ Combine the egg and milk. Add to the dry ingredients and mix well to form a soft dough. (Add a little more milk or flour if necessary.) Leave for 5 minutes. Place a large bamboo steamer (or, alternatively, place a wire cake rack in the base of a cake tin) over a pan of simmering water, not allowing the base of the steamer to touch the water.

3 ~ Lay a sheet of non-stick baking paper on the work surface and form the mixture into a roll 20 cm long. Roll in the paper and twist the ends—do not wrap it too tight as it needs to expand while cooking. Wrap the pudding in a tea towel and place in the steamer. Cover with the bamboo lid and steam for 1 1/2 hours. Check the water level, topping up with boiling water as necessary. The roll should feel firm to touch when cooked. If it still feels soft in the centre, re-cover and steam for a further 10–15 minutes, then retest. Cut into slices and serve with warm custard or cream.

NUTRITION PER SERVE
Protein 15 g; Fat 33 g; Carbohydrate 105 g; Dietary Fibre 4 g; Cholesterol 119 mg; 3248 kJ (776 cal)

Notes ~ This is an old-fashioned English pudding. It is also known as Spotted Dog or Plum Bolster.

Mix the egg and milk mixture with the dry ingredients—add extra milk if needed.

On a sheet of baking paper, form the dough into a roll.

Roll up the pudding in the baking paper
and loosely twist the ends.

Wrap the pudding in a tea towel and place
in the steamer and cover.

～ Peach Brown Betty ～

Preparation time:
20 minutes
Total cooking time:
50 minutes
Serves 4

---

170 g butter, chopped
3 cups (240 g) coarse
   fresh breadcrumbs
3/4 cup (165 g) firmly
   packed soft brown
   sugar

1/2 teaspoon ground
   nutmeg
825 g can peaches,
   drained, chopped
3/4 cup (90 g) slivered
   almonds

1.～Preheat the oven to moderate 180°C (350°F/Gas 4). In a large frying pan, melt 150 g of the butter, add the breadcrumbs and toss over medium heat until the breadcrumbs are golden brown. Combine the sugar and nutmeg.
2.～Grease a 1.25 litre soufflé dish. Place one third of the breadcrumbs over the base and top with half of the peaches, a third of the sugar mixture and half of the almonds.
3.～Repeat with a second layer and top with a final layer of breadcrumbs. Use the back of a spoon to firmly press the mixture down. Sprinkle with the remaining sugar and dot with the remaining butter. Bake for 35–40 minutes, or until golden brown.

NUTRITION PER SERVE
Protein 15 g; Fat 48 g; Carbohydrate 105 g; Dietary Fibre 7.5 g; Cholesterol 110 mg; 3745 kJ (895 cal)

Toss the breadcrumbs and butter over medium heat until golden brown.

Layer half of the peaches on top of the breadcrumb mixture.

Top with a final layer of breadcrumbs, pressing down firmly with a spoon.

Dot the remaining butter on top of the sugar layer.

～ Fig Pudding ～

Preparation time:
40 minutes
Total cooking time:
3 hours 40 minutes
Serves 8

---

500 g dried figs
1¾ cups (440 ml) milk
3 cups (240 g) coarse
  fresh breadcrumbs
¾ cup (140 g) lightly
  packed soft brown
  sugar

2 cups (250 g)
  self-raising flour,
  sifted
2 eggs, lightly beaten
150 g unsalted butter,
  melted

---

1. ～Grease the base and side of a 2 litre pudding basin with melted butter. Place a round of baking paper in the bottom of the basin.

2. ～Place the empty basin in a large pan on a trivet or upturned saucer and pour in enough cold water to come halfway up the side of the basin. Remove the basin and put the water on to boil.

3. ～Chop the figs and place in a small saucepan with the milk. Bring to a simmer, cover and cook over low heat for 10 minutes. This mixture will curdle—stir to combine.

4. ～Combine the breadcrumbs, brown sugar and sifted flour in a large bowl. Stir in the soaked figs and any liquid, the beaten eggs and the melted butter. Spoon into the basin.

5. ～Lay a sheet of foil on the work surface and cover with a sheet of baking paper. Make a large pleat in the middle. Grease the paper with melted butter. Place, paper-side-down, over the top of the basin and tie the string securely around the rim of the basin and over the top to make a handle. The string handle is used to lift the pudding in and out of the pan.

6. ～Gently lower the basin into the simmering water and cover with a tight-fitting lid. Cook for 3½ hours. Check the level of water, topping up with boiling water as necessary. The pudding is cooked when a skewer inserted in the centre comes out clean. Leave the pudding for 5 minutes before turning out. Serve with custard or cream.

NUTRITION PER SERVE
Protein 13 g; Fat 20 g; Carbohydrate 100 g; Dietary Fibre 11 g; Cholesterol 100 mg; 2645 kJ (630 cal)

Cook the figs and milk over low heat, stirring well when the mixture curdles.

Spoon the mixture into the prepared pudding basin.

～ Eve's Pudding ～

Preparation time:
25 minutes
Total cooking time:
1 hour
Serves 4–6

1.6 kg cooking apples,
  peeled and cored
2 tablespoons sugar
125 g butter, softened
1/2 cup (125 g) caster
  sugar

2 eggs
1 teaspoon vanilla
  essence
1/2 cup (125 ml) milk
1 1/2 cups (185 g)
  self-raising flour

1.～Preheat the oven to moderate 180°C (350°F/ Gas 4). Grease a deep 1.5 litre ovenproof dish.
2.～Thickly slice the apples and place in a pan with 1 tablespoon water and the sugar. Cover and cook over medium heat for 12 minutes, or until the apple is soft but still holding its shape. Spoon the apple into the dish. Leave to cool.
3.～Beat the butter and sugar until light and creamy. Add the eggs, one at a time, beating well after each addition. Fold in the vanilla essence and milk alternately with the sifted flour.
4.～Smooth the mixture over the apple. Bake for 40–45 minutes, or until a skewer inserted into the centre of the cake comes out clean.

NUTRITION PER SERVE (6)
Protein 6.5 g; Fat 2.8 g; Carbohydrate 68 g; Dietary Fibre 3.5 g; Cholesterol 65 mg; 1330 kJ (318 cal)

Peel and core the cooking apples, then slice them thickly.

Spoon the cooked apple into the greased ovenproof dish.

Add the eggs one at a time to the creamed butter and sugar mixture.

Evenly spread the pudding mixture over the apple and smooth the surface.

~ Lemon Syrup Pudding ~

Preparation time:
40 minutes
Total cooking time:
2 hours 10 minutes
Serves 6

160 g unsalted butter,
softened
1 cup (250 g) caster
sugar
2 teaspoons finely
grated lemon rind
2 eggs
2 cups (250 g)
self-raising flour
1/4 cup (60 ml) milk

1/2 cup (125 ml) lemon
juice

Lemon syrup
2 cups (500 ml) lemon
juice
1 cup (250 g) caster
sugar
4 lemons, zested
(see Note)

1. Grease the base and side of a 2 litre pudding basin with melted butter. Place a round of baking paper in the bottom of the basin.

2. Place the empty basin in a large pan on a trivet or upturned saucer and pour in enough cold water to come halfway up the side of the basin. Remove the basin and put the water on to boil.

3. Using electric beaters, beat the butter and sugar in a small bowl until light and creamy. Add the lemon rind and beat until thoroughly combined. Add the eggs one at a time, beating well after each addition. Transfer to a large bowl and, using a large metal spoon, fold in the sifted flour alternately with the combined milk and lemon juice. Spoon into the pudding basin.

4. Lay a sheet of foil on the work surface and cover with a sheet of baking paper. Make a large pleat in the middle. Grease the paper with melted butter. Place, paper-side-down, over the top of the basin and tie string securely around the rim of the basin and over the top to make a handle. The string handle is used to lift the pudding in and out of the pan.

5. Gently lower the basin into the simmering water and cover with a tight-fitting lid. Cook for 2 hours. Check the level of water, topping up with boiling water as necessary. The pudding is cooked when a skewer inserted in the centre comes out clean. Leave the pudding for 5 minutes, then pierce the base with a skewer. Turn out onto a plate and pierce all over the top and side of the pudding.

6. To make the lemon syrup, place the lemon juice, sugar and lemon zest in a small pan and stir over low heat until the sugar has dissolved. Increase the heat, bring to the boil and boil for 3 minutes. Pour half of the warm syrup over the pudding, covering the top and side. Serve accompanied by the remaining syrup and whipped cream.

NUTRITION PER SERVE
Protein 7 g; Fat 17 g;
Carbohydrate 115 g; Dietary
Fibre 1.8 g; Cholesterol 103 mg;
2680 kJ (640 cal)

Notes To zest a lemon, thinly peel off the skin, avoiding the bitter white pith. Shred finely. Alternatively, you could use a special zester. If the lemon syrup is a little too tart, adjust the sugar to your taste.

Pierce the base of the pudding with a skewer before turning out onto a plate.

A special citrus zester will help you remove the zest from the lemons quickly and easily.

～ Jam Roly Poly ～

Preparation time:
25 minutes
Total cooking time:
30 minutes
Serves 4

1½ cups (185 g)
self-raising flour
30 g butter, chopped
½ cup (125 ml) milk

½ cup (160 g) jam,
warmed
40 g butter, diced, extra
½ cup (125 g) sugar

1.～Preheat the oven to moderate 180°C (350°F/Gas 4). Grease a shallow ovenproof dish.
2.～Sift the flour into a bowl, add the butter and rub in until it resembles breadcrumbs. Make a well in the centre, add the milk and mix with a flat-bladed knife to form a firm dough. Gather the dough together and turn onto a lightly floured surface. Press into a ball and roll out to form a 20 x 25 cm rectangle. Spread with jam, leaving a 1 cm border. Roll up firmly lengthways. Trim the edges. Place into the dish, seam-side-down.
3.～Mix together the extra butter, sugar and 1 cup (250 ml) boiling water until the butter has melted and the sugar has dissolved. Gently pour the sauce over the dough.
4.～Bake for 30 minutes, or until firm to touch and the sauce has thickened.

NUTRITION PER SERVE
Protein 6 g; Fat 15 g;
Carbohydrate 90 g; Dietary
Fibre 2.5 g; Cholesterol 50 mg;
2210 kJ (530 cal)

Mix together, using a flat-bladed knife, to form a firm dough.

Spread the dough evenly with jam, leaving a narrow border.

Place the jam roll seam-side-down into the ovenproof dish.

Gently pour the sauce evenly over the dough.

~ Butterscotch ~ Self-saucing Pudding

Preparation time:
25 minutes
Total cooking time:
40 minutes
Serves 4

1¼ cups (155 g)
  self-raising flour
¼ cup (55 g) firmly
  packed soft brown
  sugar
80 g butter, melted
⅓ cup (80 ml) milk
1 egg, lightly beaten

Sauce
¾ cup (165 g) firmly
  packed soft brown
  sugar
1½ cups (375 ml)
  boiling water
40 g butter, chopped

1 ~ Preheat the oven to moderate 180°C (350°F/Gas 4). Lightly grease a 1.75 litre soufflé or deep ovenproof dish with melted butter.

2 ~ Sift the flour into a large bowl, add the sugar and stir well. Make a well in the centre of the dry ingredients. Mix together the melted butter, milk and beaten egg and pour into the well. Stir until combined, but do not overbeat. Spread the mixture evenly into the dish.

3 ~ To make the sauce, sprinkle the brown sugar over the top of the pudding mixture. Combine the water and butter, stirring until the butter has completely melted. Pour gently over the back of a spoon onto the pudding mixture. Bake for 35 minutes, or until a skewer comes out clean when inserted into the centre of the cake only—a sauce will have formed underneath. Serve warm with whipped cream.

NUTRITION PER SERVE
Protein 6.5 g; Fat 25 g; Carbohydrate 80 g; Dietary Fibre 1.5 g; Cholesterol 125 mg; 2240 kJ (583 cal)

Note ~ You can also cook this pudding in individual ovenproof dishes. Cook for 20–25 minutes, or until a skewer comes out clean.
Hint ~ Self-saucing puddings need to be served fairly soon after they are cooked, as the sauce will thicken and will soak into the cake if left too long.

Spoon the mixture into the prepared ovenproof dish.

Gently pour the liquid over the back of a spoon onto the pudding mixture.

~ Chocolate Fudge Puddings ~ with Chocolate Fudge Sauce

Preparation time:
40 minutes
Total cooking time:
45 minutes
Serves 8

150 g butter
3/4 cups (185 g) caster
  sugar
100 g dark chocolate,
  melted and cooled
2 eggs
1/2 cup (60 g) plain flour
1 cup (125 g)
  self-raising flour
1/4 cup (30 g) cocoa
  powder

1 teaspoon bicarbonate
  of soda
1/2 cup (125 ml) milk

Sauce
50 g butter, chopped
125 g dark chocolate,
  chopped
1/2 cup (125 ml) cream
1 teaspoon vanilla
  essence

1.~Preheat the oven to moderate 180°C (350°F/ Gas 4). Lightly grease eight 1 cup (250 ml) metal moulds with melted butter and line each base with a round of baking paper.

2.~Beat the butter and sugar until light and creamy. Add the melted chocolate, beating well. Add the eggs one at a time, beating well after each addition.

3.~Sift together the plain and self-raising flours, cocoa powder and bicarbonate of soda, then fold into the chocolate mixture. Add the milk and fold through. Half fill the moulds. Cover the moulds with pieces of greased foil and place in a large, deep baking dish. Pour in enough boiling water to come halfway up the sides of the moulds. Bake for 35–40 minutes, or until a skewer inserted into the centre of each pudding comes out clean.

4.~To make the sauce, combine the butter, chocolate, cream and vanilla essence in a pan. Stir over low heat until the butter and chocolate have completely melted. Pour over the pudding and serve with whipped cream.

NUTRITION PER SERVE
Protein 7 g; Fat 38 g; Carbohydrate 60 g; Dietary Fibre 1.5 g; Cholesterol 130 mg; 2490 kJ (595 cal)

Beat together the butter and sugar until the mixture is light and creamy.

Fold the flour, then the milk through the chocolate mixture.

Cover each chocolate pudding with a piece of greased foil.

Pour in enough boiling water to reach halfway up the sides of the moulds.

~ Apple Crumble ~

Preparation time:
20 minutes
Total cooking time:
45 minutes
Serves 4–6

1.6 kg cooking apples
2 tablespoons caster
  sugar

Crumble
1 cup (125 g) plain flour

¹/2 cup (95 g) lightly
  packed soft brown
  sugar
³/4 teaspoon ground
  cinnamon
100 g butter, chopped

1. ~Preheat the oven to moderate 180°C (350°F/ Gas 4). Peel and core the apples and cut each apple into 8 wedges. Place the apple in a pan with ¹/4 cup (60 ml) water. Bring to the boil, then reduce the heat to low and cover. Cook for 15 minutes, or until the apple is just soft. Stir in the sugar and spoon into a 1.5 litre shallow ovenproof dish.

2. ~Mix together the flour, brown sugar and cinnamon. Add the butter and rub with just your fingertips until the mixture resembles coarse breadcrumbs. Spread evenly over the top of the apple. Bake for 25–30 minutes, or until golden brown and crisp. Serve with cream or ice cream.

NUTRITION PER SERVE (6)
Protein 3 g; Fat 15 g;
Carbohydrate 60 g; Dietary
Fibre 3 g; Cholesterol 43 mg;
1575 kJ (375 cal)

Peel and core the apples, then cut each one into 8 wedges.

Cook the apple for 15 minutes, or until it is just soft.

Rub the butter into the dry ingredients until it resembles coarse breadcrumbs.

Spread the crumble mixture evenly over the apple.

～ Boiled Christmas Pudding ～

Preparation time:
1 hour
+ overnight soaking
+ overnight drying
Total cooking time:
7 hours
Serves 8–10

500 g mixed sultanas,
  currants and raisins
300 g mixed dried fruit,
  chopped
50 g mixed peel
1/2 cup (125 ml)
  brown ale
2 tablespoons rum
juice and rind of
  1 orange and 1 lemon
225 g fresh suet, grated
1 1/3 cups (245 g) lightly
  packed soft brown
  sugar

3 eggs, lightly beaten
2 1/2 cups (200 g) fresh
  white breadcrumbs
3/4 cup (90 g)
  self-raising flour
1 teaspoon mixed spice
1/4 teaspoon freshly
  grated nutmeg
1/3 cup (60 g) blanched
  almonds, roughly
  chopped
plain flour, to dust

1.～Place the dried fruit, mixed peel, ale, rum, orange and lemon juice and rind in a large bowl. Cover and leave overnight.

2.～Mix the fruit mixture, suet, sugar, eggs, breadcrumbs, flour, spices, almonds and 1/4 teaspoon salt in a large bowl. Leave for 10 minutes.

3.～Cut an 80 cm square from a piece of calico, or a clean old tea towel, and boil it in a pan of water for 20 minutes. Wring out (wearing rubber gloves) and spread on a clean work surface. Dust the calico with a thick layer of sifted flour, leaving a margin around the edge. Spread the flour out with your hands—it is important that you get an even covering as the flour will form a seal between the pudding and the water.

4.～Place the pudding mixture in the centre of the calico and bring the points of the material together. Gather in all the excess, making the folds neat and even. Tie the top tightly with a piece of string, leaving some room for expansion. Tie a loop in the end of one of the pieces of string and hook a wooden spoon handle through it. Lower the pudding onto a trivet or upturned saucer in a large pan of boiling water—the pan should be large enough for the pudding to move around. Cover and boil for 5 hours. Check the water level, topping up with boiling water as necessary. The pudding should not rest on the base of the pan.

5.～Remove the pudding from the water and hang it in a dry, well-ventilated area where it will not touch anything else. Make sure all the calico ends are opened out and sit loosely on top of the the pudding. Leave hanging overnight.

6.～Remove the string and, if there are still damp patches, spread the top out gently to make sure the calico dries thoroughly all over. When dry, tie with a new piece of string and store the pudding hanging in a dry, cool place for up to 4 months.

7.～To serve, boil for 2 hours as above, hang for 15 minutes and remove the cloth. Place rounded-side-up on a plate and serve with brandy butter.

NUTRITION PER SERVE (10)
Protein 8.75 g; Fat 25 g; Carbohydrate 100 g; Dietary Fibre 7.15 g; Cholesterol 70 mg; 2762 kJ (660 cal)

Using your hands, spread out an even layer of plain flour over the calico.

Gather up the excess calico, ensuring the folds are neat and even.

~ Christmas ~
Ice Cream Pudding

Preparation time:
1 hour
+ 3 nights soaking
and freezing
Total cooking time:
Nil
Serves 10

1/3 cup (50 g) almonds,
toasted and chopped
1/4 cup (45 g) mixed peel
1/2 cup (60 g) raisins,
chopped
1/2 cup (60 g) sultanas
1/3 cup (50 g) currants
1/3 cup (80 ml) rum
1 litre good-quality
vanilla ice cream

1/2 cup (105 g) red and
green glacé cherries,
quartered
1 1/2 litres good-quality
chocolate ice cream
1 teaspoon mixed spice
1 teaspoon ground
cinnamon
1/2 teaspoon ground
nutmeg

1 ~ Mix the almonds, peel, raisins, sultanas, currants and rum in a bowl, cover with plastic wrap and leave overnight. Chill a 2 litre pudding basin in the freezer.

2 ~ Soften the vanilla ice cream slightly and mix in the cherries. Press this ice cream around the inside of the chilled pudding basin, spreading it evenly right to the top of the basin. Return the basin to the freezer and leave overnight. It might be necessary to check the ice cream a couple of times and spread it again evenly to the top.

3 ~ Soften the chocolate ice cream slightly and mix with the spices. Stir in the soaked fruit and nut mixture. Spoon into the centre of the pudding basin and smooth the top. Freeze overnight or until very firm. Turn the pudding out onto a plate (cover the basin briefly with a hot towel if the pudding does not release easily). Serve cut into wedges.

NUTRITION PER SERVE
Protein 6.5 g; Fat 23 g;
Carbohydrate 45 g; Dietary
Fibre 1.29 g; Cholesterol 46 mg;
1748 kJ (417 cal)

Hint ~ You can put coins and charms into an ice cream Christmas pudding as with a traditional Christmas pudding. Wrap each one in foil and poke them into the pudding before serving. Warn your guests if you do this to avoid any broken teeth.

Mix the green and red cherries into the slightly softened vanilla ice cream.

Evenly spread the vanilla ice cream mixture to the top of the basin.

Spoon the chocolate ice cream mixture into the centre of the basin and smooth over.

Turn the pudding out onto a serving plate and cut into wedges to serve.

∼ Sauces, Custards and Toppings ∼

Sauces and custards make a delicious and subtle contribution to the pudding experience—and investing a little time into their preparation will guarantee pleasing results.

Chocolate Custard

Break 50 g dark chocolate into a pan with $1^1/2$ cups (375 ml) milk. Place the pan over low heat, stirring occasionally, until the chocolate has melted and the mixture is well combined. Whisk 4 egg yolks, $1/4$ cup (60 g) sugar, 1 teaspoon plain flour, 1 teaspoon cornflour and 1 tablespoon cocoa powder in a heatproof bowl until thick and pale. Gradually add the milk, whisking until combined. Return to the pan and stir over very low heat until the custard thickens and coats the back of a wooden spoon. Remove from the heat and stir in 1 teaspoon vanilla essence. Makes $1^3/4$ cups.

Brandy Butter

Using electric beaters, beat 250 g (8 oz) soft unsalted butter and $1^1/2$ cups (185 g) sifted icing sugar until smooth and creamy. Gradually add $1/4$ cup (60 ml) brandy, beating thoroughly. Refrigerate until required. Makes $1^1/4$ cups.

Left to right: Chocolate Custard, Brandy Butter, Whisky Sauce, Crème Anglaise and Vanilla Custard.

Whisky Sauce

Melt 2 tablespoons butter in a pan over low heat. Remove from the heat, stir in $1/3$ cup (40 g) plain flour. Mix together well. Gradually whisk in 2 cups (500 ml) milk and 2 tablespoons caster sugar. Return to medium heat and whisk until the sauce thickens and comes to the boil. Reduce the heat and simmer for 10 minutes, stirring occasionally. Remove from the heat, and stir in $1/3$ cup (80 ml) whisky, 2 teaspoons butter and 1 tablespoon double cream. Cover with plastic wrap until serving. Makes 2 cups.

Crème Anglaise

Split a vanilla bean lengthways and place in a pan with $1^1/2$ cups (375 ml) milk. Heat until almost boiling. Cover and leave to infuse for 10 minutes. Whisk 3 egg yolks and 2 tablespoons sugar for 3 minutes, or until light and creamy. Remove the bean and add the milk to the egg mixture, stirring constantly. Return to the cleaned pan and stir over low heat for 5 minutes, or until thickened and the custard coats the back of a spoon—do not boil or it will curdle. Makes $1^3/4$ cups.

Vanilla Custard

Place 1 cup (250 ml) milk and $1/4$ cup (60 ml) cream in a pan. Mix well. Bring to the boil, then remove from the heat immediately. In a bowl, whisk 3 egg yolks, $1/2$ cup (125 g) caster sugar and 2 teaspoons cornflour. Slowly pour the hot milk and cream onto the egg mixture, whisking continuously. Return to the pan and stir over low heat until the mixture boils and thickens. Remove from the heat and stir in $1/2$ teaspoon vanilla essence. Makes $2^1/4$ cups.

~ Index ~

apple Charlotte, 12
apple crumble, 56

Betty, peach brown, 42
boiled Christmas
   pudding, 58
brandy butter, 62
bread & butter pudding,
   30
brown Betty, peach, 42
butterscotch self-saucing
   pudding, 52

Charlotte, apple, 12
cherry clafoutis, 16
chocolate
   chocolate custard, 62
   chocolate fudge
      puddings with
      chocolate fudge
      sauce, 54
   chocolate self-saucing
      pudding, 4
Christmas ice cream
   pudding, 60
Christmas pudding,
   boiled, 58
Christmas pudding,
   steamed, 28
clafoutis, cherry, 16
cobbler, plum, 38
crème anglaise, 63
crumble, apple, 56
custard, chocolate,
   62
custard, vanilla, 63

dumplings, golden
   syrup, 36

Eve's pudding, 46

fig pudding, 44

fruit, dried
   boiled Christmas
      pudding, 58
   bread & butter
      pudding, 30
   Christmas ice cream
      pudding, 60
   fig pudding, 44
   spotted Dick, 40
   steamed Christmas
      pudding, 28
   sticky date pudding,
      32
fruit, fresh
   apple Charlotte, 12
   apple crumble, 56
   cherry clafoutis, 16
   Eve's pudding, 46
   lemon delicious, 6
   lemon syrup pudding,
      48
   orange marmalade
      pudding, 34
   peach brown Betty, 42
   pineapple upside-down
      cake, 18
   plum cobbler, 38
   queen of puddings, 8
   summer pudding, 26
fudge puddings,
   chocolate, 54
fudge sauce, chocolate,
   54

ginger pudding, 20
golden syrup
   dumplings, 36

ice cream pudding,
   Christmas, 60

jam puddings, 10
jam roly poly, 50

lemon delicious, 6
lemon syrup pudding, 48

marmalade pudding,
   orange, 34

orange marmalade
   pudding, 34

peach brown Betty, 42
pineapple upside-down
   cake, 18
plum cobbler, 38

queen of puddings, 8

rice pudding, 24
roly poly, jam, 50

sauce, chocolate fudge,
   54
sauce, whisky, 62
self-saucing pudding,
   butterscotch, 52
self-saucing pudding,
   chocolate, 4
spotted Dick, 40
steamed Christmas
   pudding, 28
sticky date pudding, 32
summer pudding, 26
Sussex pond pudding, 14
sweet potato pudding, 24
syrup pudding, lemon, 48

treacle pudding, 22

upside-down cake,
   pineapple, 18

vanilla custard, 63

whisky sauce, 62